Oboe Student

by
Blaine Edlefsen
in collaboration with
Fred Weber

LEV M000026312

To The Student

This book, with the aid of a good teacher, is designed to help you become an excellent player on your instrument in a most enjoyable manner. It will take a reasonable amount of work and CAREFUL practice on your part. If you do this, learning to play should be a valuable and pleasant experience.

To The Teacher

The Belwin "Student Instrumental Course" is the first and only complete course for individual instruction of all band instruments. Like instruments may be taught in classes. Cornets, trombones, baritones, and basses may be taught together. The course is designed to give the student a sound musical background and at the same time provide for the highest degree of interest and motivation. The entire course is correlated to the band oriented sequence.

To make the course both authoritative and practical, most books are co-authored by a national authority of each instrument in collaboration with Fred Weber, perhaps the most widely-known and accepted authority at the student level.

The Belwin "Student Instrumental Course" has three levels: elementary, intermediate, and advanced intermediate. Each level consists of a method and three correlating supplementary books. In addition, a duet book is available for Flute, B♭ Clarinet, E♭ Alto Sax, B♭ Cornet and Trombone. The chart below shows the correlating books available with each part.

The Belwin "STUDENT INSTRUMENTAL COURSE" - A course for individual and class instruction of LIKE instruments, at three levels, for all band instruments.

EACH BOOK IS COMPLETE IN ITSELF BUT ALL BOOKS ARE CORRELATED WITH EACH OTHER

METHOD
The Oboe Student
For individual
or
Oboe Class
instruction.

ALTHOUGH EACH BOOK CAN BE USED SEPARATELY, IDEALLY, ALL SUPPLEMENTARY BOOKS SHOULD BE USED AS COMPANION BOOKS WITH THE METHOD

STUDIES AND MELODIOUS ETUDES
Supplementary scales, warm-up and technical drills, musicianship studies and melody-like studies.

TUNES FOR TECHNIC
Technical type melodies, variations, and "famous passages" from musical literature --- for the development of technical dexterity.

THE OBOE SOLOIST
Interesting and playable graded easy solo arrangements of famous and well-liked melodies. Easy piano accompaniments.

How To Read The Chart

- ● — Indicates hole closed, or keys to be pressed.

- ○ — Indicates hole open.

■ When two ways to finger a note are given, the first way is the one most often used. The second fingering is used in special situations.

■ When two notes are given together (F♯ and G♭ for example), they sound the same pitch and are, of course, fingered the same way.

In order to make this chart as easy to understand as possible, only those fingerings necessary to play this method book are given.

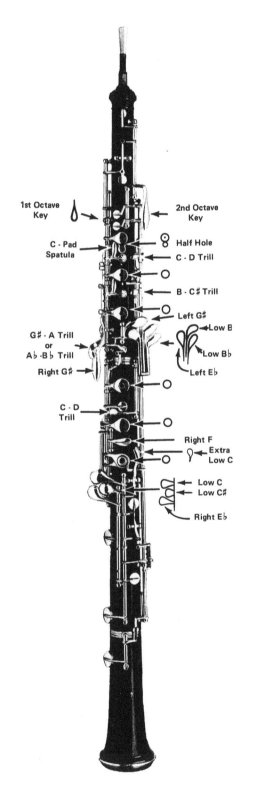

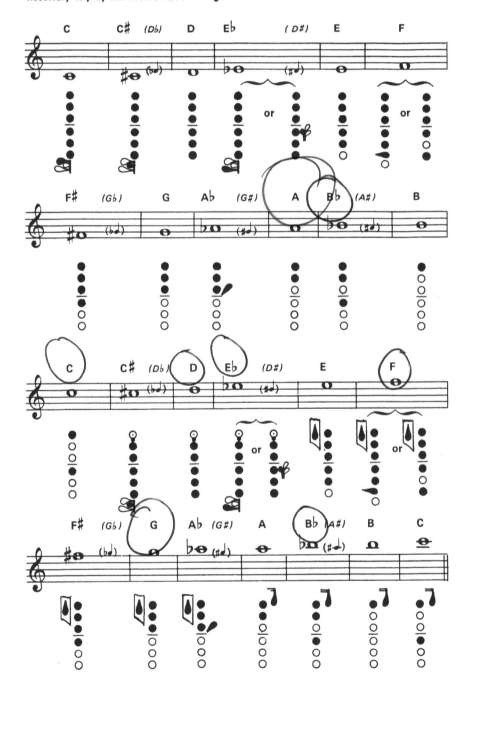

Getting Started

SETTING THE EMBOUCHURE.

Setting the embouchure described below will work well with one having normal teeth and jaw structure. Within this framework, however, certain variations are possible and often necessary.

1. Open the mouth naturally, i.e. without moving the chin forward as the jaw is lowered.

2. Place the tip of the reed on the lower lip about even with the line which separates the smooth from the somewhat rougher and dryer surface.

3. The reed is then rolled into the mouth with the lips as they are folded over the upper and lower teeth. As this is done, the ring muscle contracts and thickens to form a secure and flexible boundary for the reed blades. The ring muscle is taken into the mouth behind the upper and lower teeth. No air pockets between the gums and cheeks or lips should be allowed to form.

4. The teeth act as a support for the lips but do not exert pressure directly onto the reed. This pressure must be accomplished mainly by the lip muscles and by the lower jaw via the teeth and lips.

5. Ordinarily, only a small amount of reed, about 1/16 to 1/8 inch, should protrude into the mouth beyond the lips.

6. The front and back of the tongue are held in a position as if saying *oo* as in the word *toot*. The tongue point is always held (when not moving) very close to the end of the reed. The under-tip of the tongue may rest on top of the lower lip.

STARTING THE SOUND.

To start the sound we must (1) inhale, (2) form the embouchure for the tone desired, (3) place the very point or top tip of the tongue on the middle or a corner of the lower blade tip, (4) build up the pressure in the airway to the desired level, then (5) quickly drop the tongue tip away from the reed tip as if pronouncing the word *too*.

PRODUCING (ARTICULATING) ENDINGS OF TONES.

The articulation of tone endings is done in several ways. The two main methods are as follows:

1. We simply move the tongue point back to the reed tip corner *while maintaining constant air pressure.*

2. We move the lips tighter toward and around the reed tip while blowing less air into the reed. The breath support must remain strong as long as the tone sounds. The length of this ending is determined by the speed of the articulation.

**Right Side View Of
Embouchure And Hand Position**

**Left Side View Of
Embouchure And Hand Position**

**Front View Of
Embouchure And Hand Position**

Lesson 1   Reading Music

You should know the following rudiments before starting to play:

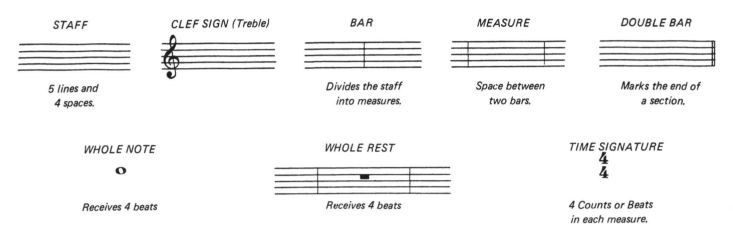

STAFF	CLEF SIGN (Treble)	BAR	MEASURE	DOUBLE BAR
5 lines and 4 spaces.		Divides the staff into measures.	Space between two bars.	Marks the end of a section.

WHOLE NOTE
o
Receives 4 beats

WHOLE REST
Receives 4 beats

TIME SIGNATURE
4
4
4 Counts or Beats in each measure.

Notes and Musical Terms used for the first time are pointed out with ARROWS.
They should be memorized.

Time Signature

SLUR: Tongue only the first note of a slur.

Let old air out first.

Leave reed on lower lip and open mouth to breathe.

Lesson 2

You are now ready to begin the companion books, STUDIES AND MELODIOUS ETUDES and TUNES FOR TECHNIC, correlated with the method as part of the BELWIN STUDENT INSTRUMENTAL COURSE.

QUARTER NOTE
1 Count

①

②

a sharp carries through the measure.

③

HALF NOTE
2 Counts

HALF REST
2 Counts

④

Finger Movement Study

Slur and Tongue Excersise   *Repeat Sign*

⑤

Repeat each section until clean.

Suggestions for moving the fingers.

1. Hold the fingers curved to avoid raising them too high.
2. Move the fingers very rapidly to and from the keys even in slow rhythm.
3. Use only enough pressure to close the keys.
4. Always move the fingers in a precise rhythm.
5. The left thumb may be held in a flexed and slightly curved position touching the oboe very lightly just below the first octave key.

⑥

Merrily We Roll Along

Play in one breath

⑦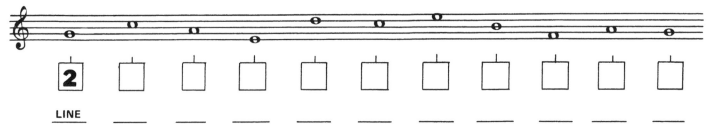

Put the number of the line or space the note is on the square and write below whether the note is on a line or space.

2

LINE ___ ___ ___ ___ ___ ___ ___ ___ ___ ___

Lesson 3

QUARTER REST
1 Count

TIE – 3 counts
(combines notes of same pitch.
Do not tongue second note.)

Write counting under the notes.

Count 1 2 3 4 1 2 3 4 1

Finger Movement Study

Slur and tongue. Play in a very precise rhythm. Use "snappy" finger movements.

Mary Had A Little Lamb

Put the following on the staff.

| Whole Note | Sharp | Quarter Note | A time Signature | Quarter Rest | Half rest | Tie Two Notes |

Lesson 4

You are now ready to play solos from THE OBOE SOLOIST, a book of solos with Piano Accompaniments correlated with the Method as part of the BELWIN STUDENT INSTRUMENTAL COURSE.

DOTTED HALF NOTE — the dot adds half of the time of the preceeding note.

Go Tell Aunt Rhode

Cross Finger Play

Counting Fun

A-Tiskit A-Taskit

Counting Duet

Put the note called for on the correct line or space used so far in this book.

Example:	Whole Note on B	Half Note on C	Quarter Note on F	Dotted Quarter on A	Whole note on G	Quarter Note on E	Half Note on D

Lesson 5

Comparing C (Common) And ₵ (Cut) Time

1 Count 1 2 3 4 1234 1 2 3 4 1234

2 1 + 2 + 1 + 2 + 1 + 2 + 1 + 2 +

Lightly Row

3 Practice in C and in ₵ .

Yankee Doodle

Key signature: this means all F's are played F#.

4 Top line of the staff is also F.

Natural cancels the effect of a # or ♭ .

Using The Right Hand F Key

5 F♮

Right hand F key. → Slur then tongue. ⓐ ⓑ

6 To remind you

7

8

Merrily We Roll Along

9

At Pierrot's Door

10

① Put names of notes in squares above the staff. **②** Fill in correct fingerings.

Lesson 6

Lesson 7

Small R means use right f key. ➤ R

① C / C key ➤

②

The Cuckoo

③

C Major Scale

HOLD — give extra length

④

⑤

Hold each note as long as possible for practice.

March Time

$\frac{2}{4}$ *TIME — 2 counts per measure.*

⑥

Small R means use right f key.

*Alternate Use Of Forked-F And Right Hand F Key

⑦

⑧

*Note: Most fine professional oboes have a left hand f key. If your oboe has such a key, you should practice playing notes marked **F** with the left hand f key and forked **F** throughout the entire book.*

A-Tiskit, A-Taskit

⑨

Write the note receiving the number of counts called for in $\frac{4}{4}$ time.

1	3	2	4	3	1	2	4	3	2	4	2	1	3	1	2	4

Lesson 8

Lesson 9   *Playing The Half Hole Fingering*

A SUGGESTED PROCEDURE:

Playing the half-hole is done by rocking or rolling the first finger of the left hand off and onto the perforation in the B key. Do not lift the finger from the key during either movement. Keep the finger in a curved shape at all times, i.e. with the nail-middle-and knuckle-joints bent. Do not extend or contract the finger during these movements. The movements are made only at the knuckle joint by increasing and decreasing the spread between the first and second fingers. A sliding movement or a combination of sliding and rocking movements is a more advanced technique which one can develop later. In the beginning stages, simply rock or roll the finger.

Counting Tune

London Bridge

Put in the bar lines.

Lesson 10

Half Hole Study

Bicycle Built For Two

Mary Had A Little Lamb Duet

(Study both parts.)

Billy Boy

Important Exercises

In the following exercises, neither forked f's nor right hand f's are marked. First mark the F's; F for forked or R for right, then practice the exercise. From this point on, fewer forked and right hand f's will be marked.

Lesson 11

Using The First Octave Key

Suggestions: The left thumb should always rest with almost no weight on the instrument. To play the first octave key you may lift the thumb off and then move it to the end of the key. You may also slide or rock the thumb on and off.

Octaves

Finger Movement Studies

Fanfare

Duet For Counting

(Study both parts.)

Forked-F Duet

Half Hole Rock

* Suggestions: On these wide ascending intervals, roll the reed farther into the mouth. For the wide descending intervals, roll the reed out of the mouth. Do not drop your jaw. Do not let the reed slip in and out of the mouth; we simply roll it.

Lesson 12

Combining The Half Hole And First Octave Key Movements

On Top Of Old Smokey

Caisson March

Count 𝄴 3 4 1 2 3 4 1 etc.
Count 𝄵 2 + 1 + 2 + 1

Study In G Major

Study In F Major

Use right hand F key throughout.

Write the counting under the measures below.

15

Lesson 13

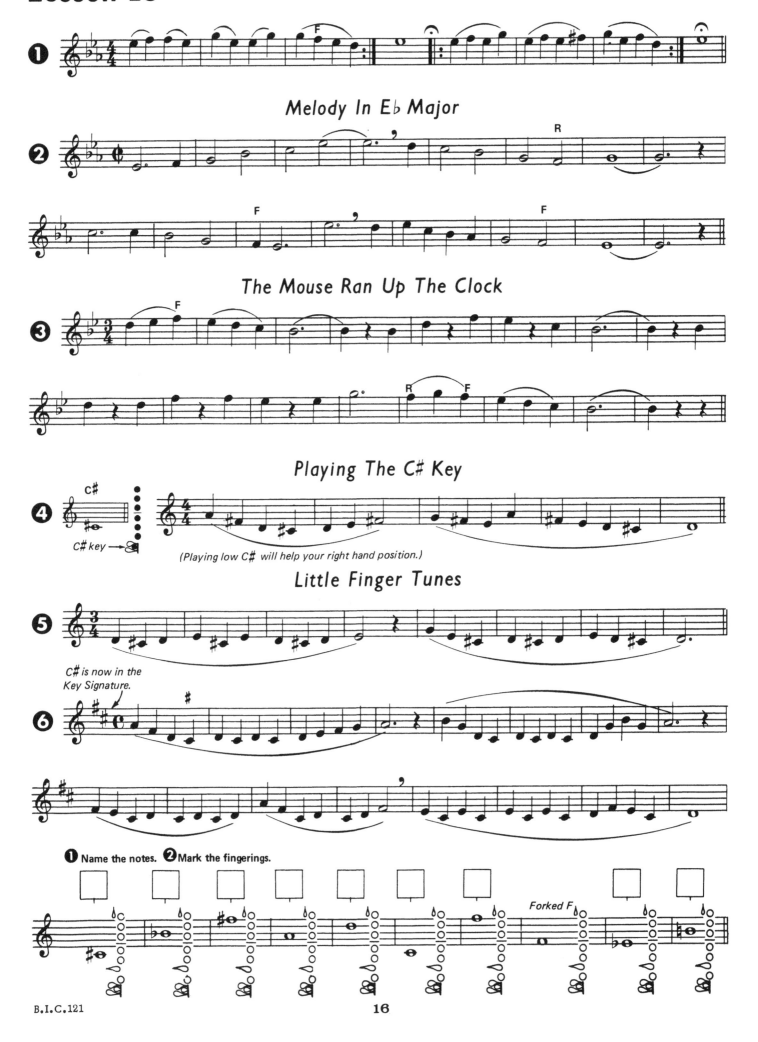

Melody In E♭ Major

The Mouse Ran Up The Clock

Playing The C♯ Key

(Playing low C♯ will help your right hand position.)

Little Finger Tunes

C♯ is now in the Key Signature.

❶ Name the notes. ❷ Mark the fingerings.

Forked F

Lesson 14

Hold each note as long as possible.

Apply to scale to low D and back to high G.

Faith Of Our Fathers

Play all F's forked.

Forked-F Study

In finger movement studies such as this one, the tempos may be slow, but the finger movements must always be extremely quick and snappy.

Where Has My Little Dog Gone

Chromatic Waltz

Tongue also.

Fine
(End or Finish)

D.C. al Fine
(means repeat from beginning to Fine.)

On the space provided, mark N OK, for those notes using no octave key, HH for those using half hole, and F O K for those using the first octave key.

Lesson 15

① *Thirds*

Slur the two ways marked, then tongue each note.

②

③

Abide With Me

④

Repeat both ascending and descending intervals several times to make smooth

⑤ C♯ (D♭)

O How Lovely Is The Evening Duet

⑥

First oboist plays notes with stems up.
Second oboist plays notes with stems down.

Variations On A Familiar Tune

C♯ in Key Signature.

⑦

Like B♭ .

Fill in the bar lines.

Lesson 16

Eighth Notes

① 𝄞 **C** or 𝄵
  C = 1 2 3 4 etc.
  𝄵 = 1 + 2 + etc.

② 𝄞 2/4
  Count 1 + 2 + 1 + 2 + 1 + 2 + 1 + 2 +

③

④ Slur as marked, then tongue each note.

Tongue repeated notes within a slur, unless they are tied.

R R F R

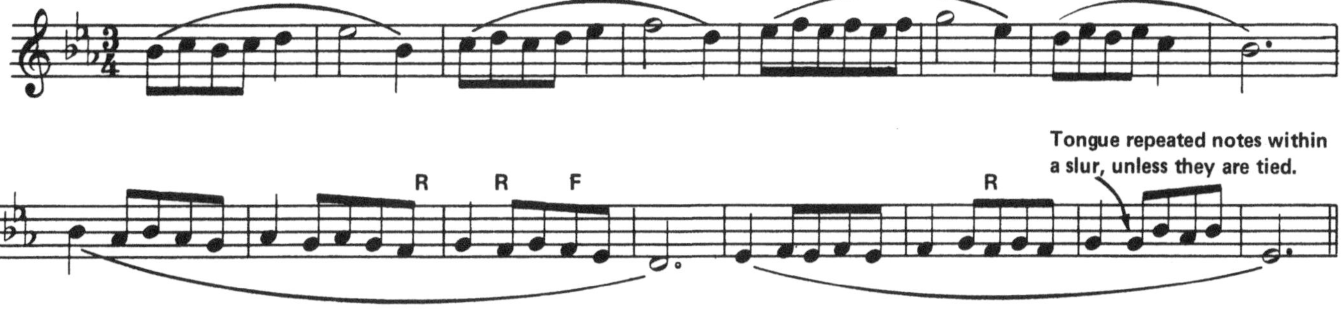

Jingle Bells

⑤

Skip To My Lou

⑥ F R

R

I Was Born About 10,000 Years Ago

⑦ 
Count 4 + 1 + 2 + etc.

Lesson 17

Controlling Loudness For More Expressive Playing

f   stands for *FORTE* which means play loudly.
mf stands for *MEZZO FORTE* which means play moderately loud.
p   stands for *PIANO* which means play softly.

1. To play softer move the lips tighter around the reed and toward the reed tip.
2. Playing louder is done the opposite way.
3. Hold each tone steady. Make good beginnings and long endings.

Counting Fun

Johnny Has Gone For A Soldier

Lesson 18

1st time: *f*   *f*   *f*   *f*   *f*   *f*   *f*   *f*
2nd time: *mf*   *mf*   *mf*   *mf*   *mf*   *mf*   *mf*   *mf*
3rd time: *p*   *p*   *p*   *p*   *p*   *p*   *p*   *p*

Apply to the scale descending and ascending at all three loudness levels.

Forked-F Speed Test

Test your speed for each line. Passages must be clean.

Captain Kidd

She'll Be Comin' 'Round The Mountain

Count   2   +   1   +   2   +

Lesson 19

Scale Review

Scale of F Major.

Scale of D Major.

Scale of C Major.

Scale of Bb Major.

Scale of G Major

Octaves

Are You Sleeping, Brother John?

A FRENCH ROUND

In a round, two or more voices play the same melody starting at different times. Ask your teacher how this round works.

Scale of Eb Major.

Lesson 20

The Eighth Rest

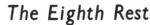

EIGHTH REST

❶ Count   1 + 2 +   1 + 2 +

STACCATO MARK means play
notes detached or separated.

❷

The notes in measures 1 + 2 should be about the same length. Dotted notes are somewhat shorter than those without dots.

Good King Wenceslas

ENGLAND

❸

❹

Ab(G#)

A Theme From The Opera, "The Magic Flute"

Slowly

W. A. MOZART

❺

Etude In C Major

❻

Lesson 21

Diminuendo Study

This means DIMENUENDO (dim.) — play gradually softer.

Apply to scale.

Duet In Spanish Style

Practice both parts.

Chromatic Study

Play top octave on repeat only.

same fingering

same fingering

Merry Widow Waltz

Lesson 22

Crescendo Study

Very slow

①

$p < f$ $p < f$ $p < f$ $p < f$ $p < f$ $p < f$ $p < f$ $p < f$

← means CRESCENDO (cresc.) — play gradually louder.

$p \underline{\hspace{2cm}} f$ $p \underline{\hspace{2cm}} f$ *simile* ← means continue in a like manner.

Apply to the scale.

Using The Second Octave Key

Second Octave Key

A

②

Suggestions: To play the second octave key, simply rotate the forearm. Do not bend the wrist or change the curve of the of the fingers. Keep the elbow the same distance from the body.

③

Dotted Quarter Notes

④

Count 1 + 2 + 3 + 4 + 1 + 2 + 3 + 4 +   *simile*   1 + 2 + 3 + 4 + 1 + 2 + 3 + 4 +   *simile*

America, The Beautiful

⑤

All Through The Night

⑥

Hymn Of Thanks

⑦

Lesson 23

Using The Second Octave Key

Follow On Duet

Chromatic Study

Streets Of Laredo

Lesson 24

① Very slowly

f > p < f > p < f *simile to G*

Very slowly

← Breathe after two measures.

f > p < f > p < f

Apply to scale above.

Combining First Octave Key And Second Octave Key Movements

Suggestion: Always play the octave keys separately, that is, play only one octave key at a time.

② Slow

ⓐ ⓑ ⓒ ⓓ

Auld Lang Syne

Tongue repeated notes in slurs unless they are tied.

③

Short'nin' Bread

④

C Major Scale—Two Octaves

2nd OK (octave key)
1st OK
hh (half hole)
hh
1 OK
2 OK

⑤

Chromatic Study

1 OK
hh
2 OK
1 OK
hh

⑥

Lesson 25

Play like 2 staccato eighths.

Combining First And Second Octave Key Movements

Remember — Play only one octave key at a time.

Swiss Walking Song

Johannes Brahm's Lullaby

Lesson 26

Chromatic Study

Chromatic Waltz

(Practice lower octave first) Reminder: Play only one octave key at a time.

Sweet Nightingale

ENGLAND

Deck The Halls

WELSH CAROL

Lesson 27

30

Lesson 28

Playing The Left Hand E♭ -D# Key

1. The left hand E♭ -D# key is used in fingerings which come before or after those requiring the low C or C# key.

2. Playing the left hand E♭ key will help you develop the correct hand position.

Left hand E♭ -D# Key

Use left hand E♭'s + D#'s.

Lesson 29

1 Slow

f p f p   *f p f p*   *f p f p*   *f p*   *f p f p*   *f p f p*   *f p f p*   *f p*

⁶⁄₈ Time

⁶⁄₈ TIME equals 6 eighth notes per measure.

♪ = 1 Count,   ♩ = 2 Counts.   ♩. = 3 Counts,   ♩ = 6 Counts.

Aria Theme From Verdi's Opera, "Aida"

2 Moderately slow

R   R

Count 1 2 3 4 5 6   1 2 3 4 5 6   *p*   *mf*   *f*   *mf*
p

R   F   F

f   *dim.*   *p*

A Frog He Would A-Wooing Go

3

R   R

Count   6   1 2 3 4 5 6   1 2 3 4 5 6   *simile*

R   R

1 2 3 4   5

Key Of A♭ Major

D♭ now in the Key Signature.

4   F L   L   R   R   L   L   R

Vive l' Amour

5   1   2   UNITED STATES

Children's Prayer From The Opera, "Hansel And Gretel"

E. HUMPERDINCK

6

Lesson 30

Accents

Play measures 1 and 2 alike.

To accent, play louder during the first part of the tone than during the last part. Accented tones are louder than unaccented ones.

1 ——→ — receives 1 count.
2 ——→ — receive 1 count.
4 ——→ — receive 1 count.

Sixteeth Notes

Count   1   +   2   +   comes in the middle of the beat.

Left Hand Eb - D# With Half Hole
(For practice, use all left hand Eb's.)

Eb D#

Use left hand Eb

Use left hand Eb before and after Db.

Prayer Of Thanksgiving

Db now in the Key Signature

Key of Ab Major.

Listen To The Mocking Bird

HAWTHORNE

Count   4   +

Lesson 31

Ten Little Indians

Finger Movement Studies

Variation On "Grandfather's Clock"

Lesson 32

Aꞵ Major Scale And Arpeggio

Theme From The Tone Poem, "Finlandia"

JEAN SIBELIUS

Lesson 33

Minuet

WOLFGANG AMADEUS MOZART
(1756 - 1791)

Piece In G Minor

Piece In A Minor

Slur two ways

A Legend

PETER TSCHAIKOWSKY, Op. 54, No.5

Moderately

Basic Technic

To play from low Db to C or low C to Db, play Db with the ball of the finger, the low C with the flat part.

Stepwise scale Play all scales connected (legato) staccato, and as marked by your teacher.

Key name?

Scale in Thirds

ARPEGGIOS

Key name?

Half Hole Review

Repeat each measure until clear and clean.

* Practice left hand as well as right hand Eb - D#.

B.I.C.121

Basic Technic

Stepwise scale

Key name?

Play all scales legato, staccato, and as marked by your teacher.

Scale in thirds.

ARPEGGIOS

Combining The First Octave Key and Half Hole Movements

(Use right E♭ also.)

Key name?

Forked-F Study

Play all f's forked for practice.

Play both octaves.

Basic Technic

Stepwise scale

Key name?

1

Play all scales connected (legato) staccato, and then as penciled in by your teacher.

Scale in thirds.

ARPEGGIOS

Combining The First And Second Octave Key Movements

2

Play both octaves

Key name?

3

Combining The Half Hole And The Second Octave Key Movements

Legato (connected)

4

Key name?

5

Speed Test

Name the notes. Work for speed. Each test should be completed in 1 minute and 30 seconds or less. When completed turn the page upside down and try again.

Completed in ___ Seconds.

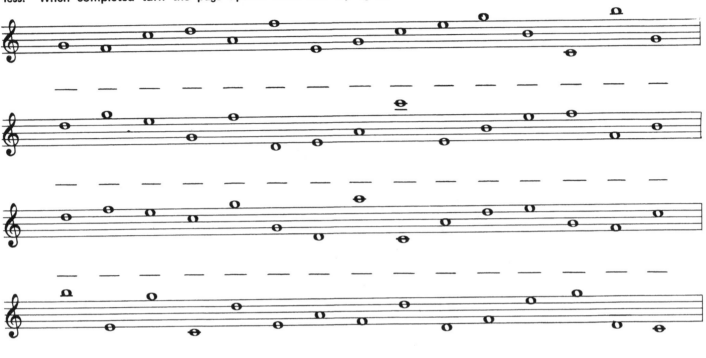

Home Practice Record

Week	Mon.	Tues.	Wed.	Thurs.	Fri.	Sat.	Total	Parent's Signature	Week	Mon.	Tues.	Wed.	Thurs.	Fri.	Sat.	Total	Parent's Signature
1			Class	15					21								
2									22								
3									23								
4									24								
5									25								
6									26								
7									27								
8									28								
9									29								
10									30								
11									31								
12									32								
13									33								
14									34								
15									35								
16									36								
17									37								
18									38								
19									39								
20									40								